COWBOYS OF THE OLD WEST
COLORING BOOK

David Rickman

Dover Publications, Inc., New York

For Guy, Ben and Emily Ravey,
who are still young enough to dream

Acknowledgments

I would like to thank those who were instrumental in inspiring and assisting me to complete this book. Above all I am grateful to my wife, Helen K. Davie, who, as always, has drawn on her own talents as illustrator and writer when reviewing my work. I would also like to thank Diane and David Baltzer, Jeff and Joel Harris, Mark Tovar, and Mike Olivari and his horse Arby, who generously served as my models. Finally I would like to thank Hopalong Cassidy and Roy Rogers for being my first heroes.

D.R.

Copyright © 1985 by David Rickman.
All rights reserved under Pan American and International Copyright Conventions.

Published in Canada by General Publishing Company, Ltd., 30 Lesmill Road, Don Mills, Toronto, Ontario.
Published in the United Kingdom by Constable and Company, Ltd.

Cowboys of the Old West Coloring Book is a new work, first published by Dover Publications, Inc., in 1985.

DOVER *Pictorial Archive* SERIES

This book belongs to the Dover Pictorial Archive Series. You may use the designs and illustrations for graphics and crafts applications, free and without special permission, provided that you include no more than four in the same publication or project. (For permission for additional use, please write to Dover Publications, Inc., 31 East 2nd Street, Mineola, N.Y. 11501.)

However, republication or reproduction of any illustration by any other graphic service whether it be in a book or in any other design resource is strictly prohibited.

International Standard Book Number: 0-486-25001-6

Manufactured in the United States of America
Dover Publications, Inc., 31 East 2nd Street, Mineola, N.Y. 11501

Introduction

Altogether cowboys are a large-hearted class of fellows . . . the constant communication with nature . . . the days and nights of lonely cruising and camping on the prairie, the uninterrupted communion with and study of self which this occupation affords, tends to make young men honest and noble.

G. SHIELDS, author, 1886

Some of my experiences were going hungry, getting wet and cold, riding sore-backed horses, going to sleep on herd and losing cattle, getting cussed by the boss, scouting for gray-backs [body lice], trying the sick racket now and then to get a night's sleep. . . . I put in eighteen or twenty years on the trail and all I had in the final outcome was the high-heeled boots, the striped pants, and about $4.80 worth of other clothes, so there you are.

G. O. BURROWS, ex-cowboy, 1924

The American cowboy is both a myth and a reality. All of us know the myth—a symbol of the United States recognized around the world, an image used to sell everything from canned prunes to after-shave. As a class, cowboys have been said to represent every human quality from untarnished virtue to absolute depravity; businessmen, statesmen, farmers and truck drivers all claim a piece of the cowboy "spirit." And yet close inspection of the original article reveals every aspect of this mythical image to be fanciful. Today the handful of men still employed as full-time cowboys speak reverently of "keeping the cowboy tradition alive," perhaps not realizing that it is the myth they are sustaining and not the reality.

Cowboys have a very long history, but throughout most of it few of them would have had any idea what was meant by a tradition, since their world was evolving and carrying them with it. The classic era of cowboys took place west of the Mississippi and east of the Rockies from 1865 to 1885 and was a time of unfenced range, booming beef prices and long cattle drives. Yet the history of cowboys covers much more time and much more territory.

Every cowboy should trace his profession's history back further than those twenty years of the nineteenth century. It begins with the arrival of the first cattle and the introduction of the horse into the New World by Columbus and Cortés. In Mexico the Spanish ranching culture, already strongly influenced by the Moors, was further changed by the strange conditions of a new land and by the use of herdsmen of African and Native American ancestry. These herdsmen, called "vaqueros," moved the cattle and horses northward to establish stock-raising in the American Southwest. The coming of the Texans and other ranchers from the United States brought further changes to the Spanish heritage during the years of slow growth in Texas before the Civil War. Boom years for the West followed the war, and mythical cowboy heroes entered the popular culture. Later, despite the collapse of the cattle boom and the end of the open range, ranching survived and so did the cowboy. More important, the mythical cowboy also survived, in novels, plays, advertising, paintings, Wild West shows and, finally, the cinema.

Yet in all this history, where is the source of the "American cowboy" of popular image to be found? Everywhere, in that elements from all his ancestors went into making the present-day image. Nowhere, in that with so many centuries, cultures, locations and individuals, it is impossible to generalize about cowboys without backtracking to explain the exceptions.

Try, for example, to describe the historical cowboy in one sentence. You might say he was a man on horseback who tended cattle with a lariat. The part about cattle is generally true, but in their long history, cowboys have also herded sheep, goats, pigs and even geese and turkeys. The lariat was not perfected until three centuries after Columbus; at various times and places, lances, tridents, hocking knives, as well as lassos tied to a horse's tail or hung on a long pole, were used for the same job. Horseback? Many cattlemen have done their work on the back of a mule, or on foot, and bull riders in modern rodeos are still certain to call themselves cowboys. As for being a man, there were many examples of women cowhands and ranchers who did their jobs well.

Though the cowboy of the mythical sort is always white and usually born and raised in Texas, real cowboys over the centuries were of every conceivable origin. Mexicans and blacks have long played a major role, comprising no less than a third of the cowboy population after the Civil War. Native Americans were among the first cowboys, having received their training at Spanish missions, and continue to contribute first-class ranch hands. Immigrants from almost every European nation became cowboys. Among them were some well-educated men from families with wealth and titles. In the Pacific states there were even a few vaqueros of Japanese descent. The term "American cowboy" may in fact be more accurate than we realize, since cowboys have certainly lived up to the American motto, *e pluribus unum*.

Not even the word cowboy can be used without explanation. It originated centuries ago in Ireland and was used during the American Revolution and in early Texas to mean cattle thieves. Many men have rejected the word in describing themselves, and others in their time never heard of it. Vaquero is the term that the Mexicans and Southwesterners first used. In Texas even many of the non-Hispanic cattlemen—both white and black—preferred to be called vaqueros. Riders in the Pacific Slope region used vaquero and later buckaroo. Nineteenth-century writers usually hyphenated the word, as cow-boy, and did not commonly use it until after the Civil War. Elsewhere in the West, cattlemen clung to local terms such as puncher, drover and waddy in defiance of those who would lump them together with cowboys.

There have long been attempts to distinguish between cowboys and buckaroos. Both have the same Hispanic heritage, dating back to Columbus. Their cattle, horses, equipment, clothing and open-range methods of keeping livestock all came originally to them from Mexico. But the styles of roping, riding, equipment and clothing were said to distinguish a buckaroo (whose range included the Pacific states, Idaho, Nevada and Hawaii) from the cowboy (whose area was Texas and the Great Plains). Along the border between the two groups (the states of Arizona, New Mexico, Colorado and Wyoming), the distinction began to blur. With the advent of Wild West shows, rodeos, motion pictures and mail-order catalogues, the distinction grew hazier, generally emphasizing the cowboy, until recently, when buckaroos began to come back in fashion.

With all of these variations, what do the modern cowboy's many ancestors have in common? One thing, certainly: hard and usually thankless work. Even during the brief "classical age" of the trail drive, there were few cowboys who could see past the endless routine—riding, roping, branding, doing chores, rescuing livestock or slaughtering them—to find anything romantic in their lives. During cattle drives a man might spend two or three months on the trail, have a short binge in a ramshackle cow town, return home broke and usually spend the winter months washing dishes or doing other odd jobs in town before the next spring roundup.

Few men spent their lives as cowboys. Most lasted only a year or two before quitting to find work of some equally mundane but less hazardous sort, such as working for the railroad, tending a saloon or running a store. Many quit to get married or start their own ranches. Those who lasted past thirty were often so injured, or "stove up," from the job that they could no longer do the work, and so hung on as cooks.

Not until Eastern newspapermen traveling west on the railroad in search of new stories and new heroes "discovered" the cowboys did the legend-building begin. Something in their descriptions of cowboys, or in the cowboys themselves, caught the American imagination and never let go. Soon the dime novels that the newspaper articles inspired found their way west and into the hands of the cowboys themselves. Only then did the cowboy begin to see himself as anything other than someone just trying to get by.

Since that time the legend has continued to grow. From Owen Wister's buckskin saints and Frederic Remington's and Charles M. Russell's men of leather and steel through William S. Hart, Tom Mix and the films of John Ford and John Wayne to the humorous cowboys, the singing cowboys, the secret-agent cowboys, the television horse operas and foreign "spaghetti" Westerns right up to today, the mythical cowboy has taken on so many guises that he has proven impossible to dismiss. The legend, like those who inspired it, is a survivor.

1. Hispaniola, 1494. The American cowboy is a descendant of the stockmen who came with Columbus on his second voyage to the New World. On ranches established in Caribbean islands such as this one were raised the horses and cattle that would later be transported to Mexico by Cortés, from there to spread out over the American West. These first cowboys were heirs to a mixed Spanish and Moorish heritage, which was reflected in clothing and horse equipments, especially the *jineta*-style saddle. Before the invention of the lariat, a trident-tipped lance was used to drive cattle or to knock them down for branding.

2. Mexico, 1540. Two years after Cortés began the conquest of Mexico, the first cattle were brought to the mainland of the Americas and stock-raising began. The conquistadors were awarded grants of land, and Indians became the first ranch hands. These Indians, who were themselves branded if prisoners of war, soon became skilled stockmen. In 1540, when Coronado led his expedition to the Southwest, he took cattle and horses with him from the vast herds of Mexico. In these early days of ranching two styles of riding were in use; *jineta*, a Moorish style whose saddle was shown in the previous illustration, and *la brida*, whose heavier "war" saddles are shown here.

3. Mexico, early seventeenth century. It is impossible to say when the lariat was invented, but by the seventeenth century it was definitely in use in Mexico. At first it was a crude affair: very thick rawhide cord tied to the horse's tail, neck or saddle girth and dropped over the intended animal's head by using a stick. It would then take a skilled rider to whip the rope around his victim's hindquarters to trip it. If this was not done quickly an enraged horse or bovine could easily injure or kill the vaquero.

4. Mexico and the Southwest, 1598. The first permanent introduction of Spanish livestock into the Southwest was in the colony of New Mexico led by Juan de Oñate. Inventories of his expedition note horses, sheep, goats and two types of cattle. The true "Texas" longhorn actually originated in Texas from a mix of these two kinds of cattle; the more common variety were beef and work animals of the sort still found in Spain and Portugal, while the others were the famed Spanish fighting bulls. Both types of animals prospered so well in Texas that they were impossible to contain and in a few generations spread in immense wild herds. By the late sixteenth century the Mexican vaqueros, commonly of black and Indian as well as Spanish heritage, often mixed elements of *jineta* and *la brida* riding together, an evolution that would lead to today's Western riding style.

5. Arizona, 1687. From the sixteenth to the nineteenth centuries a great chain of Catholic missions was established throughout the Spanish-American empire. Many of these became great ranches that used Indians to tend the herds. In the Southwest generally, this plan had mixed success. For various reasons, including poor land and the independent spirit of the Indians, most of these enterprises failed. In Arizona, however, the Jesuit fathers were successful in their efforts. The padre-vaquero shown here carries a pole tipped with a hocking knife, which was used to down cattle by hamstringing them, before they were slaughtered. His saddle is of European design and carries what appears to be a roping horn, despite the fact that it was not yet used for roping.

6. Baja California, 1769. By the mid-eighteenth century, stock-raising was well established in Lower California, and from there moved north. As yet the hazardous innovation of roping had not been fully developed, and in many regions the vaqueros preferred to throw cattle by using a lance or a hocking knife or by skillfully flipping the animal over by its tail. Despite the lack of roping, horns were common features on saddles.

7. California mission vaquero, late eighteenth–early nineteenth centuries. Beginning in 1769 the Franciscan friars began establishing missions along the coast of California. Despite the fact that Spain had a long-standing prohibition against allowing Indians to ride, the padres throughout the colonies ignored the rule because they needed hands to maintain the growing mission herds. In a short time the missionaries transformed hunters and gatherers into expert vaqueros. About this time it became common to use the saddle horn for roping.

8. Californios, 1826. Following Mexican independence, the Catholic missions in California were closed; their lands and herds were snatched up by the ranchers, who grew wealthy selling cattle hides and tallow to merchant sea captains calling at the coast. For a short while this was an age of huge estates, wealthy dons and gracious living. A popular sport of the vaqueros was roping grizzly bears, which abounded in California. The outfits of these riders are typical of the time, as is their horse equipment, heavy leather *mochilas* over wooden saddletrees. The rider in the background carries *armas*, coverings for the legs that later developed into chaps.

9. Texas, 1833. The earliest American settlers to enter Texas brought with them a few shorthorn cattle and a very different approach to stock-raising. Settling mostly in the wooded eastern part of Texas, these Texans (or "Texians," as they called themselves) slowly adapted to the conditions by farming and ranching. It appears that because men already knew how to farm, it was left to the women to learn how to ranch, and in most families men only helped out at roundups. At this time, Hispanic saddles and methods of stock-handling had limited use among the Texans.

10. California, 1846. The golden age of rancho life ended with the Mexican War. Yankee newcomers began taking from the Californios the land which they, in turn, had originally taken from the Indians. With the passing of the great estates went the gracious living and fine clothes. Here, in their last splendor, a man and woman in riding clothes share a corn-shuck cigarette. The vaquero on horseback is wearing *armitas*, the earliest form of the true chaps.

11. Texas, 1830s–1840s. During their war for independence and after, Texans calling themselves "cow-boys" began entering the prairies and plains of western Texas in search of cattle. Between the Nueces and Pecos rivers they found vast herds, some wild and others the property of Spanish-speaking Texans. The Texans gathered both and built great herds of their own. Though as yet the Texan could not claim to be as skillful a vaquero as the Mexican, he had begun to adopt some of the gear, including the lariat and the "skeleton-rigged" saddle.

12. New Mexico, 1846. Because of rugged conditions and the lack of a ready market, cattle-raising was not as profitable in the Southwest as it was in California. To make ends meet a vaquero might also hunt buffalo, trade with the Comanches or guard the caravans that traveled to St. Louis and California. A typical horseman of this land might wear a well-made poncho belted at the waist for warmth, a glazed sombrero and leather trousers and leggings—on his back an Indian-made bow, widely used since firearms were scarce.

13. Texas, 1854. Rich now in cattle, but with no one to buy them, the Texans began undertaking trail drives over stupendous distances in search of a market. New Orleans was an unprofitable destination since the route lay through swampland, yet many herds were trailed there. By the early 1850s the route to Missouri was well established, and some herds went on to Chicago; one trail driver even took a herd overland to New York City. With the California Gold Rush, a new market was opening up. The risks were great but so were the profits, and for almost ten years herds traveled regularly to the gold fields. The men who drove the herds called themselves vaqueros and included not only Hispanics but blacks, whites and even Delaware Indians.

14. California and the Far West, 1850s. Though demand for beef in the California and Colorado gold fields was great, the Texan drives faced competition from closer rivals: Californian vaqueros, augmented by new, non-Hispanic horsemen, made epic drives of their own across uncharted lands; on the northern plains, new herds were established to serve this same market. While the Texans could be identified at a glance by their "skeleton-rigged" (almost bare) saddles, the horsemen of the Far West continued to use the *mochila*-covered saddles with only slight modifications, such as leather underskirting.

15. Texas, 1860. From the days of the Spanish, the West was rich in horses but, seemingly, short of time. Though there were kinder ways of taming horses, vaqueros and cowboys commonly used methods that were cruel, but effective: choking, beating and spurring usually brought obedience. These methods were hard on horses, yet they took a much greater toll on men. Ruptures, broken bones, lost teeth and often enough death were the price paid for a string of "well-broke" horses.

16. Texas, the Civil War. Since almost all of the able-bodied young men went off to war, the work of managing the huge herds was carried on by boys, slaves, women and old men. By this time the Texans, still not completely comfortable with the lariat, had developed distinctive methods of catching and holding cattle. Often dogs were used to grab cattle by the ear or lip and hold them until a man could come with a rope. Calves could be thrown by hand, but older cattle were often tied to a tree and then tripped. Metal rings and bars were the common branding irons of the day. To protect himself from brush, the man shown here wears leggings of cowhide with the hair left on.

17. A trail herd, 1867. Following the war, Texas' fortunes were revived by a growing market for beef. The railroad made it possible to transport live cattle to the Chicago slaughterhouses; the meat could then be sent eastward to the great cities in refrigerated cars. To get to the railheads the Texan ranchers and their men drove herds averaging 2,500 head northward. Facing months of tedious work and hardship required strong, loyal men. To make their lives somewhat easier, the rancher Charles Goodnight invented the "chuck wagon" in 1866 to carry the food and the men's personal belongings.

18. South Texas, 1866. Texan ranchers returning home after the Civil War organized "cow hunts," as roundups were called then, to reestablish the scattered herds. Others without ranches built herds from unmarked cattle, or turned rawhider, genuinely "hunting" for cattle to take their hides. These were rugged times, when almost everything was homemade by a people who were especially highly skilled with rawhide.

19. Cattle town, 1870. At the end of the trail lay the railhead, where the cattle were loaded on trains for market. Boomtowns like Wichita, Abilene and Dodge City grew up almost overnight to take advantage of so many men being far from home with large amounts of money. After months on the trail and with their wages in their pockets, the "cow-boys" usually made their first stop at the bathhouse and barbershop. They then went to the clothing store, where they bought everything new and, if possible, extravagant. Finally, they set out to "paint the town red," doing their best to spend all of their wages before heading back home.

20. The northern ranges, 1871. The small ranches established before the Civil War in Wyoming and Colorado had stayed relatively small during the immediate postwar years. But booming beef prices and the demand for cattle to feed the growing mining and logging camps brought ranching to the rich grasslands of the northern ranges. After 1870, huge herds were driven north from Texas, and many of the cowboys accepted offers to stay on in the log-cabin ranch houses to tend the cattle.

21. Texas, 1876. Though nothing so rigid as a "code of the West" ever existed, certain standards of behavior were expected from a cowboy in order to make life easier for his companions. A cowboy treated "ladies" with far more care than he did the other women he met in the cow towns. To avoid dangerous rivalries, a cowboy was expected never to speak to his boss's wife or daughters unless spoken to and to avoid them whenever possible. He was free to court the women of a neighboring ranch, however, and a cowboy usually did a good deal of traveling on his day off just to visit his intended.

22. Texas-Oklahoma Panhandle, 1885. In the era of unfenced range, twice each year (spring and autumn) a harvest of cattle took place. On the southern ranges the autumn roundup was used simply to mark unbranded cattle, while the gathering in the spring saw not only marking but also the selection of adult cattle for the trail drive. Cowboys of Texas and the Great Plains still preferred to throw calves by hand, literally wrestling them to the ground. By this time, however, they no longer needed to tie the fully grown cattle to trees before tripping them, having become much more skillful with the lariat.

23. Southwest Texas, 1880s–90s. In the brush country along Texas' border with Mexico, a different sort of cattleman evolved whose work in the cactus and thorn thickets earned him the name "brush popper." Usually the brush was so thick and full of thorns that a man rode more alongside his horse than upright. A mistake at such times could mean disaster. Both man and horse emerged from a day's work of hunting wild cattle, if they were lucky, merely scratched, tattered and studded with thorns. In the brush country the cattle were unusually canny and pugnacious, often lying in ambush for the riders.

26. Winter, 1885–86. The winter months were always hard on the northern ranges, and many punchers would drift down to warmer climes to avoid them. Most ranch owners kept muskrat-fur caps and buffalo coats for the cowhands to encourage them to stay on. "Riding line" to inspect the barbed-wire fences became a common occupation as more and more ranches in the early 1880s adopted the new invention. This was the end of the open range and almost the end of ranching in the West; during the vicious winter of 1886, thousands of cattle piled up against the wire fences as they tried to escape the snow, and died.

27. Ranching women, 1880–1900. No one called them "cowgirls" then. They were the wives and daughters of ranchers, at times ranchers themselves. Doing "a man's job," but without pay, they helped when there was a shortage of cowboys or no money to pay them. These were Victorian times; a sign of this was the difficulty women faced in finding working clothes that were both practical and "decent." Despite the image from movies, few women felt comfortable with men's clothing and experimented with divided skirts, skirts with trousers and various other garb.

28. The Pacific Slope, 1880–1900. Descended from the California vaquero, the buckaroo maintained many of the Hispanic traditions that the cowboy did not. The buckaroos' style
of saddle, with its "center-fire" girth, and their style of roping have already been mentioned.
Other distinguishing characteristics were the narrow-brimmed hat, fur-covered chaps (or, in
some cases, the lighter leather *armitas*, now called "chinks"), a longer rope made of rawhide,
and the love of ornamentation on both horse and rider.

29. Oklahoma, 1890. A sadly ironic transformation took place in the West as Indian lands were cleared of both buffalo and Indians to make room for the white man's cattle: many Indians became cowboys. They worked on ranches in the Indian Nation and on other outfits throughout the West. These native cowboys formed a small but skillful corps of ranch hands and maintain this tradition even today.

30. Mexico, 1900. In Mexico the rangeland culture had continued to evolve (without the great pressures seen in the United States) right through the nineteenth century. Some felt that the evolution was progressing too rapidly, however, and by 1875 well-to-do horsemen formed *charro* societies to help codify and preserve the centuries-old culture of horsemanship and equipment. In many parts of the Southwest, Mexican and American horsemen crossed over the border to work on each other's ranches.

31. Cowboy and cowgirl, 1910. While artists and authors were trying to capture and preserve the Old West for Eastern audiences, the real West continued to evolve. Free range had been a thing of the past for a generation. Many of the best cowboys had joined Wild West shows, traveled the rodeo circuit or performed before motion-picture cameras. The notion of the "cowgirl" was developed by these show-business institutions out of Western women who knew how to rope and ride.

32. Rodeo, 1925. The origins of the rodeo are legitimate. They began in the Southwest as competitions of roping and riding usually held after the roundup. By the 1880s they were common, as entertainments, throughout the West on the Fourth of July. By the early twentieth century, however, for many cowboys they had become a substitute for ranching. Stunts like trick roping and bulldogging that had been developed by Wild West shows became regular events at rodeos. With ever larger prizes given, cowboys became professional athletes competing with speed and endurance never expected of the old-time cowboys.

33. Montana, 1939. The American demand for beef ensured that ranching would survive the disasters of the 1880s, the end of the open range and, later, even the Great Depression. Modern cowboys had new methods of keeping cattle—including grazing on public lands and systems of pens, chutes and feedlots—that would have surprised an earlier generation. Many ranches supplemented their incomes by entertaining "dudes" on vacation. The look of the cowboy was changing too. Few distinctions remained between cowboy and buckaroo: they roped differently but rode the same low, swell-forked, double-girth saddle, wore the same jeans and work clothes.

34. The B-movie hero, 1940. Though Hollywood has never made an accurate film about the era we call the Old West, it has given us the peculiarly American genre known as the Western. In countless low-budget films a basic set of morality plays has been acted out, with endless variations and ever-increasing emphasis on action. In the thirties and forties, Westerns developed a unique subgroup of films by creating an on-screen world that combined modern technology (cars, airplanes) with selected elements of the past (horses, guns). The heroes of these dramas, generally very big men on very big horses, were dressed in outfits completely unsuited to outdoor life.

35. Rodeo bull rider, 1960. Rodeos have taken on great importance to modern-day ranching, as entertainment; as a way of maintaining social ties with other ranchers, now that roundups have all but disappeared; and as a rite of passage for cowboys, now that there are no more trail drives. Events that cowboys of the last century would have tried perhaps once, on a bet, have now become institutions that are seriously discussed. By the late fifties and early sixties the distinctive look of the cowboy was "pegged" jeans that were seldom tucked into the low-heeled, pointed boots, "Western"-cut shirts, narrow kerchiefs tied to one side and a low-crowned hat with a rolled brim. Among older cattlemen this look persists to this day.

36. Buckaroo, 1985. Recently there has been a revival of interest—among the remaining handful of full-time cowboys as well as among the legions of those who wish they were—to maintain the "traditions" of the cowboys of the last century. This does not, of course, mean that authenticity is now allowed to interfere with practicality or personal taste, but some things have been revived. Mustaches, beards and long hair have come back, as have old-fashioned spurs and bits and the habit of tucking the pant leg into the boot top. One could not, however, mistake a modern cowboy for his ancestor, since he is likely to wear a down-and-nylon vest, a rodeo belt buckle, decoratively stamped boots and even a baseball cap. And this is how it should be. A look over the shoulder to the past is fine, but it is more than the old-time cowboy would have done.

37. Parade cowboys, 1985. Despite predictions of the "disappearing cowboy," though he will continue to dwindle it is unlikely that he will ever completely disappear; too many people still want to be one. Some people's idea of what a cowboy should look like, however, seems curious. At almost any American parade today one can see people dressed in creations of glitter, stainless steel, plastic and feathers, people who would, if asked, say they were dressed up as cowboys. And indeed they are, for in American culture the right of each person to claim a piece of the cowboy myth and to make it his own has become far more important than the historical reality.

DOVER COLORING BOOKS

LITTLE MERMAID COLORING BOOK, Thea Kliros and Hans Christian Andersen. (27130-7) $2.95

EXPLORATION OF NORTH AMERICA COLORING BOOK, Peter F. Copeland. (27123-4) $2.95

WILD ANIMALS STAINED GLASS COLORING BOOK, John Green. (26982-5) $3.95

HISTORIC HOUSES OF NEW ENGLAND COLORING BOOK, A. G. Smith. (27167-6) $2.95

FRENCH ALPHABET COLORING BOOK, Nina Barbaresi. (27247-8) $2.50

SPANISH ALPHABET COLORING BOOK, Nina Barbaresi. (27249-4) $2.50

SHIPWRECKS AND SUNKEN TREASURES COLORING BOOK, Peter F. Copeland. (27286-9) $2.95

SLEEPING BEAUTY COLORING BOOK, Grimm Bros. & Thea Kliros. (27318-0) $2.95

ALPHABET HIDDEN PICTURE COLORING BOOK, Anna Pomaska. (27261-3) $2.50

CALIFORNIA MISSIONS COLORING BOOK, David Rickman. (27346-6) $2.95

BUTTERFLIES COLORING BOOK, Jan Sovak. (27335-0) $2.95

INDIAN TRIBES OF NORTH AMERICA COLORING BOOK, Peter F. Copeland. (26303-7) $2.95

BIRDS OF PREY COLORING BOOK, John Green. (25989-7) $2.95

LIFE IN ANCIENT EGYPT COLORING BOOK, John Green and Stanley Appelbaum. (26130-1) $2.95

WHALES AND DOLPHINS COLORING BOOK, John Green. (26306-1) $2.95

DINOSAUR ABC COLORING BOOK, Llyn Hunter. (25786-X) $2.50

SHARKS OF THE WORLD COLORING BOOK, Llyn Hunter. (26137-9) $2.95

FUN WITH OPPOSITES COLORING BOOK, Anna Pomaska and Suzanne Ross. (25983-8) $2.50

DINOSAUR LIFE ACTIVITY BOOK, Donald Silver and Patricia Wynne. (25809-2) $2.50

THE VELVETEEN RABBIT COLORING BOOK, Margery Williams and Thea Kliros. (Available in United States only). (25924-2) $2.95

COLUMBUS DISCOVERS AMERICA COLORING BOOK, Peter F. Copeland. (25542-5) $2.95

STORY OF THE AMERICAN REVOLUTION COLORING BOOK, Peter Copeland. (25648-0) $2.95

HORSES OF THE WORLD COLORING BOOK, John Green. (24985-9) $2.95

WILD ANIMALS COLORING BOOK, John Green. (25476-3) $2.95

Paperbound unless otherwise indicated. Prices subject to change without notice. Available at your book dealer or write for free catalogues to Dept. 23, Dover Publications, Inc., 31 East 2nd Street, Mineola, N.Y. 11501. Please indicate field of interest. Each year Dover publishes over 200 books on fine art, music, crafts and needlework, antiques, languages, literature, children's books, chess, cookery, nature, anthropology, science, mathematics, and other areas.

Manufactured in the U.S.A.